TRAUMA IS REALLY STRANGE.

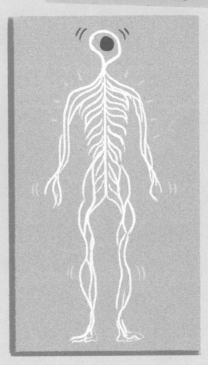

DAVID LIVINGSTONE IS MAYBE THE ULTIMATE VICTORIAN HEROIC EXPLORER. CHECK OUT HIS MANLY MUSTACHE.

'I HEARD A SHOUT; STARTING AND LOOKING HALF AROUND I SAW THE LION JUST IN THE ACT OF SPRINGING UPON ME… GROWLING HORRIBLY CLOSE TO MY EAR, HE SHOOK ME AS A TERRIER DOES A RAT. THE SHOCK PRODUCED A STUPOR SIMILAR TO THAT WHICH SEEMS TO BE FELT BY A MOUSE AFTER THE FIRST SHAKE OF THE CAT.'

'IT CAUSED A SORT OF DREAMINESS IN WHICH THERE WAS NO SENSE OF PANIC OR FEELING OF TERROR.'

SQUEEZE ANY HUMAN BEING HARD ENOUGH AND THEY WILL DISAPPEAR.

THE DREAMY, STUPOR STATE IS DISSOCIATION, AN IMMOBILIZATION OR FREEZE RESPONSE. DISSOCIATION IS ONE OF THE STRANGE THINGS ABOUT TRAUMA.

IF IT CAN HAPPEN TO OUR HERO FRIEND, IT CAN HAPPEN TO YOU.

This is a classic description of dissociation from David Livingstone, writing in 1857 (Kandel et al 2000). Leading trauma specialist Bessel van der Kolk (2014) states 'Dissociation is the essence of trauma.' After a traumatic event people often drift in and out of dissociation.

James Rhodes (2015), pianist and sexual abuse survivor, states dissociatio[n] is 'The most serious and long-lasting of all the symptoms of abuse...eve[r] since then, like a Pavlok puppy, the minute a feeling or situation eve[n] threatens to become overwhelming, I am no longer there.'

THE GOAL OF THIS BOOK IS TO BE A NON-SCARY INTRODUCTION TO TRAUMA. FOR MANY PEOPLE, UNDERSTANDING WHAT THE BRAIN IS TRYING TO DO TO PROTECT THEM HELPS HEALING.

MOST OF THE BITS OF THE BRAIN THAT DEAL WITH OVERWHELMING EVENTS ARE VERY OLD. SOME OF THE REFLEXES WE USE TO RESPOND TO DANGER ORIGINATED IN REPTILES.

IN FIGHT-OR-FLIGHT, RESOURCES SUCH AS OXYGEN, BLOOD AND SUGAR ARE DIVERTED TO THE BIG MUSCLES AND THE BRAIN. PRIMITIVE REFLEXES TAKE OVER.

'GET ME OUT OF HERE NOW!'

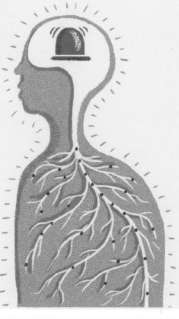

FIGHT-OR-FLIGHT OR DISSOCIATION SWITCH ON REALLY REALLY REALLY QUICKLY. UNLESS THEY ARE DISCHARGED, THE BRAIN CAN DEFAULT TO THESE LIFE AND DEATH SCENARIOS LONG AFTER THE DANGER HAS PASSED.

THIS IS THE BIG PROBLEM OF TRAUMA.

THE EXCITING NEWS IS THAT THEY CAN ALSO SWITCH OFF REALLY QUICKLY - EVEN IF THEY HAVE BEEN STUCK IN PLACE FOR YEARS.

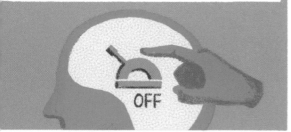

WE ALL HAVE WITHIN US THE ABILITY TO ENDURE, RECOVER AND LEARN FROM OVERWHELMING EVENTS.

common response is contracting to make ourselves small, ultimately into immobile, fetal position. We are left bracing ourselves against life, connected from our internal and external worlds. 'Trauma occurs when event creates an unresolved impact on an organism' (Levine 1997).

Running away from a lion is life or death. All non-essential activity is switched off, there is no need for digestion, libido and reproduction, immune system, or growth and repair (Sapolsky 2004). Health can dramatically improve when the 'defense cascade' is reset (Kozlowska et al 2015).

LET'S LOOK AT SOME STATEMENTS FROM CLINICAL PRACTICE THAT DEMONSTRATE THE STRANGENESS OF TRAUMA.

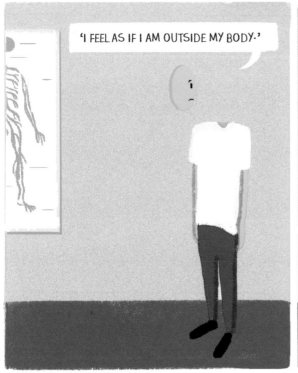

'I FEEL AS IF I AM OUTSIDE MY BODY.'

'MY LEGS ARE TINY AND FAR AWAY.'

ALSO, DISSOCIATION…

CAN MAKE US…

A BIT CLUTZY!

WE LOSE CONNECTION WITH OUR BODY OR PARTS OF OUR BODY. IT IS HARD TO STAY PRESENT AND GROUNDED.

DISSOCIATION CAN BE TERRIFYING, BUT IT CAN ALSO BE VERY HARD TO SPOT. THE CENTRAL FEATURE IS THAT BRAIN IS IN THE HABIT OF NOT FEELING.

FEEL ME

DISSOCIATION IS DIFFICULT TO IDENTIFY AS 'WE DON'T KNOW WHAT WE DON'T KNOW.' OLD PARTS OF THE BRAIN ARE TRYING TO STOP US SENSING, DISTANCING US FROM THE BODY AND LIMITING OUR PERCEPTION.

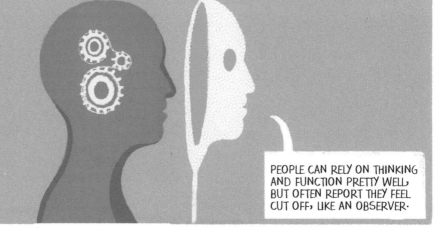

PEOPLE CAN RELY ON THINKING AND FUNCTION PRETTY WELL, BUT OFTEN REPORT THEY FEEL CUT OFF, LIKE AN OBSERVER.

'I CAN'T GET ENOUGH AIR IN.'

'THERE IS A KNOT OF ANXIETY IN MY BELLY.'

'THOUGHTS KEEP INVADING ME, IT'S AN OBSESSION I CANNOT LET GO OF.'

'I CAN'T KEEP STILL, MY MIND IS RACING.'

THESE STATEMENTS DESCRIBE BEING STUCK IN THE GO QUICK, FIGHT-OR-FLIGHT MODE.

THE BODY FEELS AS THOUGH EVERYTHING IS GEARED UP FOR ACTION. ALL THE TIME. NON-STOP. PANIC ATTACKS AND/OR RAGE ARE THE LAST STOPS ON THIS ROUTE.

Classic post-traumatic stress disorder (PTSD) symptoms include involuntarily re-experiencing aspects of the traumatic event in a very vivid and distressing way, avoidance behaviour, hyperarousal and emotional numbing (NICE 2005).

Being stuck in fast forward can be very productive. There are ma successful executives whose internal state drives them forward. But th imperative from the body is ultimately very draining and frequent associated with massive anxiety.

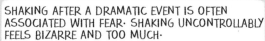

SHAKING AFTER A DRAMATIC EVENT IS OFTEN ASSOCIATED WITH FEAR. SHAKING UNCONTROLLABLY FEELS BIZARRE AND TOO MUCH.

'I'M SHAKING, IS THIS NORMAL?'

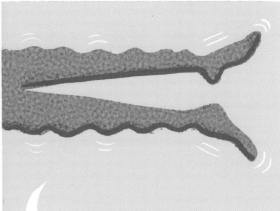

RESTLESS LEGS AND TENSION SHAKES ARE VERY COMMON WHEN WE ARE OVERWHELMED.

LETTING OURSELVES SHAKE CAN BE A VERY POWERFUL TOOL AND CAN BE USED LIKE A SAFETY VALVE TO CLEAR EXCESS ENERGY. WE CAN LEARN TO INTERACT WITH SHAKING, RATHER THAN TRYING TO DAMPEN IT DOWN ALL THE TIME. SHAKING CAN BE UNCOUPLED FROM EMOTIONAL INTENSITY.

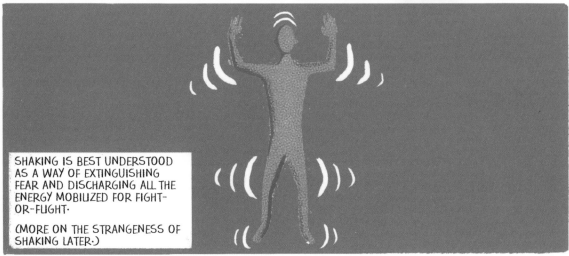

SHAKING IS BEST UNDERSTOOD AS A WAY OF EXTINGUISHING FEAR AND DISCHARGING ALL THE ENERGY MOBILIZED FOR FIGHT-OR-FLIGHT.

(MORE ON THE STRANGENESS OF SHAKING LATER.)

The 'I'm shaking, is this normal?' quote is from a young girl after watching her first deer be killed. Her dad does an amazing job of reassuring her and helping her discharge, check YouTube: 'Savannah's first deer hunt'.

The amount of people who experience restless leg syndrome (RLS) is surprisingly high: 'RLS affects 5%–10% of adults in the general population, and is associated with various chronic conditions' (Li et al 2013).

> WE CAN USE THREE STATEMENTS TO HELP UNDERSTAND WORKING WITH AND OVERCOMING TRAUMA.

1. 'THERE IS TRAUMA.' TERRIBLE THINGS HAPPEN TO HUMAN BEINGS.

TSUNAMI

WAR

2. 'WE CAN OVERCOME TRAUMA.'

WE ARE 'WIRED TO SURVIVE'. WE WOULD NOT BE HERE AS A HUMAN SPECIES UNLESS WE HAD EVOLVED WAYS OF RECOVERING FROM THAT LION ATTACK (OR SUDDEN LOSS OF A LOVED ONE, OR BEING ABUSED, OR BEING IN AN ACCIDENT...).

3. 'HEALING TRAUMA IS ABOUT MEETING THE BODY.' IN TRAUMA, OLD PARTS OF THE BRAIN CHANGE HOW THE BODY WORKS. BY PAYING ATTENTION TO FEELINGS IN THE BODY AND LEARNING TO SELF-REGULATE WE CAN REBOOT THE BRAIN.

REBOOT

'As I learned more about how people manage to withstand extremely aversive events, it became all the more apparent to me that humans are wired to survive. Not every-body manages well, but most of us do' (Bonanno 2010).

These three statements are drawn from the work of Dr David Berceli, creator of Trauma Releasing Exercises (TRE). The body is central to healing, as often 'there are no words to describe the depth of human experience the trauma survivor has been plunged into' (Berceli 2008a).

'THERE IS TRAUMA.' A REALLY FLEXIBLE TRAUMA DEFINITION IS 'ANYTHING THAT OVERWHELMS OUR ABILITY TO COPE.'

TRAUMA IS ABOUT OUR RESOURCES BEING EXCEEDED. THERE IS NO MAGIC SCALE OF EVENTS WE SHOULD MEASURE OURSELVES AGAINST. THE GREATER OUR RESOURCES THE GREATER OUR RESILIENCE.

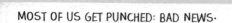

MOST OF US GET PUNCHED: BAD NEWS.

A BOXER GETS PUNCHED: ALL IN A DAY'S WORK.

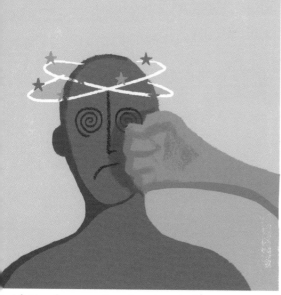

e definition of trauma is drawn from the work of trauma expert Peter vine (1997). Defining trauma is complex and political. van der Kolk 014) describes a battle to get the diagnosis PTSD accepted by American ychiatrists in the 1980s.

van der Kolk (2014) is scathing on the failure to include 'Complex PTSD' and 'Developmental Trauma Disorder' in diagnostic manuals. PTSD descriptions focus on sudden threatening events and injury, with consequences of intrusive thoughts, avoidance behaviour and increased arousal.

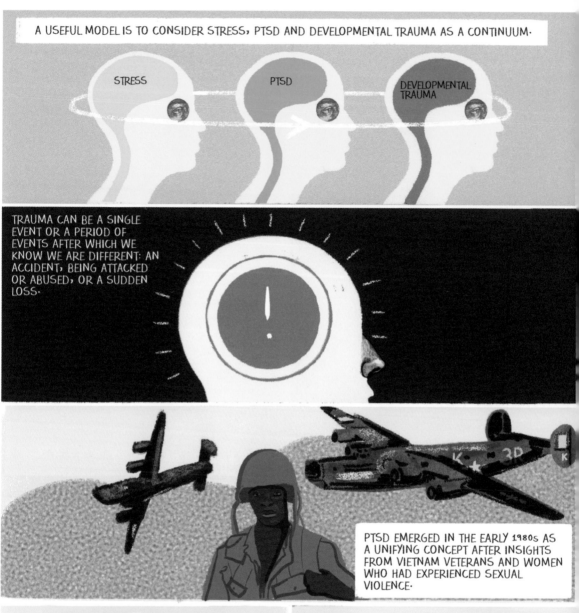

A USEFUL MODEL IS TO CONSIDER STRESS, PTSD AND DEVELOPMENTAL TRAUMA AS A CONTINUUM.

STRESS

PTSD

DEVELOPMENTAL TRAUMA

TRAUMA CAN BE A SINGLE EVENT OR A PERIOD OF EVENTS AFTER WHICH WE KNOW WE ARE DIFFERENT: AN ACCIDENT, BEING ATTACKED OR ABUSED, OR A SUDDEN LOSS.

PTSD EMERGED IN THE EARLY 1980s AS A UNIFYING CONCEPT AFTER INSIGHTS FROM VIETNAM VETERANS AND WOMEN WHO HAD EXPERIENCED SEXUAL VIOLENCE.

JAN	FEB	MAR	APR	MAY	JUNE	JUL
AUG	SEPT	OCT	NOV	DEC		

ANY DEFINITION OF TRAUMA NEEDS TO ALLOW FOR ACCUMULATED OVERWHELM, WHICH CAN OCCUR OVER A PERIOD OF TIME. SUSTAINED, EARLY DISTRESS CAN HAVE DEVASTATING CONSEQUENCES.

THE TERM 'DEVELOPMENTAL TRAUMA' RECOGNIZES THAT GROWING BRAINS ARE MORE VULNERABLE. EARLY EVENTS LEAVE DEEP IMPRINTS THAT INCREASE THE COMPLEXITY OF HEALING AND FINDING SAFETY.

'For every soldier who serves in a war zone abroad, there are ten children endangered in their own homes' and 'The consequences of caregiver abuse and neglect is vastly more common and more complex than the impact of hurricanes or motor vehicle accidents' (van der Kolk 2014).

In the space of a short comic book it is hard to do justice to the many terrible things that can overwhelm human beings. Focusing on our resilience and ability to endure is in no way meant to underplay the suffering and complexity of surviving intense fear, helplessness or horror.

FINANCIAL WORRIES, A DIFFICULT BOSS, ARGUING IN YOUR FAMILY, PUSHING TOO HARD AT THE GYM AND, BANG, WE ARE OVERLOADED AND COLLAPSE. UNBEARABLE STRESS SENDS OUR PHYSIOLOGY DOWN THE SAME ROUTE AS IF WE WERE ESCAPING A LION.

THE LINK BETWEEN DEVELOPMENTAL TRAUMA, PTSD, AND BEING STRESSED TO BREAKING POINT IS THAT THEY ALL TRIGGER THE SAME PHYSIOLOGICAL ALARM SYSTEMS.

WE SHOULD SEE TENSION, STRESS AND TRAUMA AS INTERCONNECTED.

THIS IS IMPORTANT AS MANY PEOPLE WHO ARE EXPERIENCING SIGNS OF BEING OVERWHELMED HAVE NO OBVIOUS EVENT THEY CAN PINPOINT.

THE CAUSE IS LOST IN THE PAST AND THEIR COMPLEX RANGE OF EXPERIENCES.

BUT LIFE FEELS MORE OF A STRUGGLE THAN IT SHOULD.

other cause of overwhelm: people such as family members, carers, social rkers, therapists, or first responders to emergencies can experience carious trauma' as they observe, empathize with and mirror the pain of ers (Figley 2005).

'The stress-response can become more damaging that the stressor itself.' Stress-related diseases and 'psychological uproar' emerge by continually turning on 'a physiological system that has evolved for responding to acute physical emergencies' (Sapolsky 2004).

IT IS HOPEFULLY CLEAR BY NOW THAT TRAUMA CAN BE DUE TO MUCH MORE THAN SINGLE DRAMATIC EVENTS.

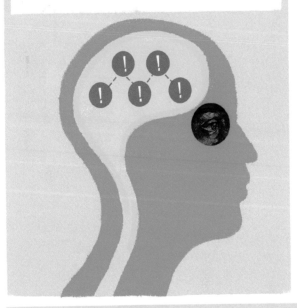

SOME OF OUR MOST IMPORTANT EXPERIENCES OCCURRED BEFORE WE WERE ABLE TO MAKE CLEAR MEMORIES.

BEING BORN MAY BE ONE OF THE TOUGHEST THINGS YOU EVER DID.

BIRTH IS AN EARLY DEFINING STORY THAT LEAVES AN IMPRINT THAT IS OUTSIDE OF CONSCIOUS AWARENESS.

BEING BORN CAN BE A JOYFUL COMING INTO POWER.

BUT FREQUENTLY IT CAN BE A STRUGGLE, WHERE IMPRINTS OF FIGHTING, BEING STUCK, DISPPEARING OR NOT GETTING THE RIGHT HELP ARE ENCODED IN OUR BODY INTELLIGENCE.

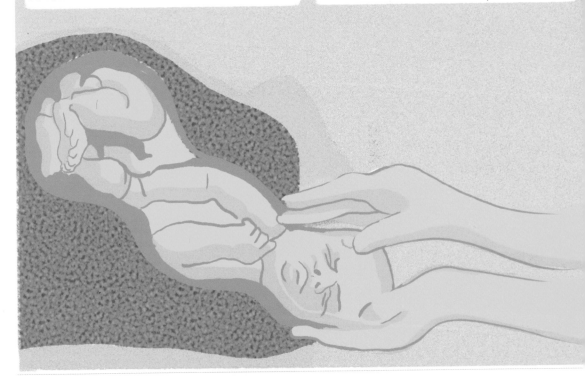

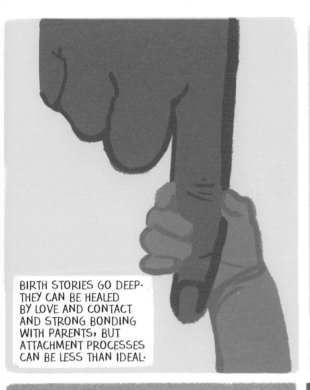

BIRTH STORIES GO DEEP.
THEY CAN BE HEALED
BY LOVE AND CONTACT
AND STRONG BONDING
WITH PARENTS, BUT
ATTACHMENT PROCESSES
CAN BE LESS THAN IDEAL.

DEVELOPMENTAL STORIES, FROM IN UTERO
AND BIRTH ONWARDS, ARE A HUGE UNKNOWN
THAT SHAPE OUR EXPERIENCE.

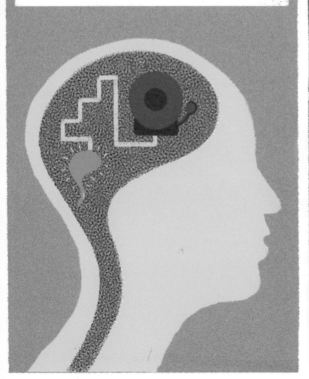

HOW WE BLINDLY FIRST RESPONDED TO EARLY
EVENTS BECOMES THE DEFAULT FOR HOW WE
RESPOND IN THE FUTURE.

BRAINS ARE SIMPLE LIKE THAT.

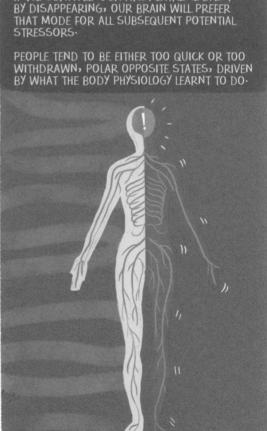

IF WE SURVIVED OUR FIRST EXTREME EVENT
BY DISAPPEARING, OUR BRAIN WILL PREFER
THAT MODE FOR ALL SUBSEQUENT POTENTIAL
STRESSORS.

PEOPLE TEND TO BE EITHER TOO QUICK OR TOO
WITHDRAWN, POLAR OPPOSITE STATES, DRIVEN
BY WHAT THE BODY PHYSIOLOGY LEARNT TO DO.

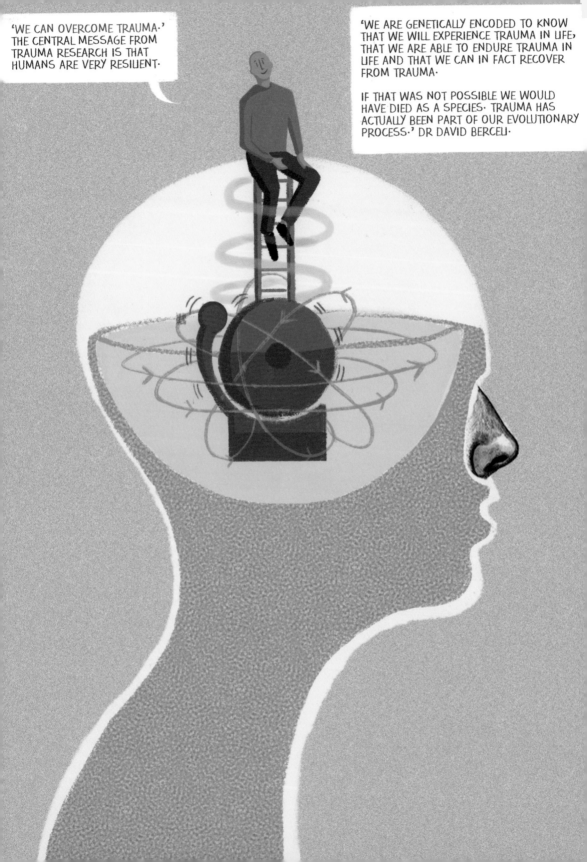

STUDYING COMMUNITIES OR GROUPS
AFFECTED BY A SINGLE DISASTER, IT HAS
BECOME CLEAR THAT 9 OUT OF 10 PEOPLE
WILL NATURALLY LEARN AND GROW
FROM THE EXPERIENCE.

THE INITAL FOCUS ON
SIMPLY DEFINING AND
RECOGNIZING PTSD HAS
SHIFTED TO MODELS OF
'POST-TRAUMATIC
GROWTH', WHERE MOST
OF US ARE TEMPERED IN
THE FIRE OF EXPERIENCE.

WE CAN, AND FREQUENTLY
DO, EMERGE STRONGER
AND WISER AFTER BEING
OVERWHELMED.

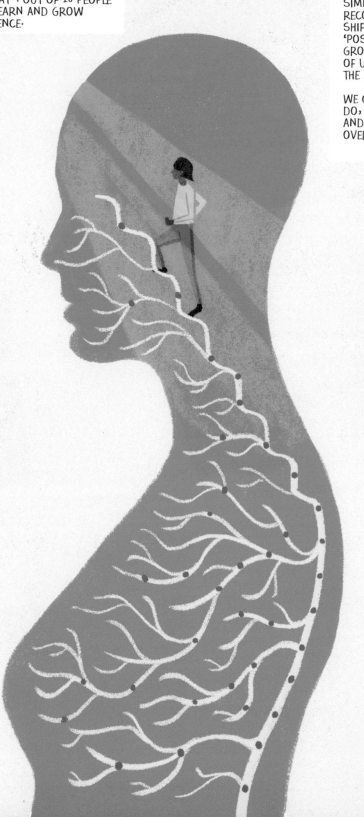

'HEALING TRAUMA IS ABOUT MEETING THE BODY.'

IT IS OFTEN NOT ENOUGH TO RECALL WHAT HAPPENED, OR TO EXPRESS EMOTION. THESE CAN BE USEFUL STEPS, BUT ARE NOT ESSENTIAL.

WHAT IS ESSENTIAL FOR TRAUMA RESOLUTION IS TO CHANGE THE BODY PHYSIOLOGY.

IN TRAUMA THE BRAIN IS ACTING TO PROTECT US AS IF THE TRAUMA IS STILL HAPPENING, RIGHT NOW.

THE AIM IS TO CHANGE THESE OVERACTIVE REFLEXES IN THE PRESENT MOMENT. THE GOAL IS NOT TO GO BACK INTO THE PAST TO CHANGE MEMORIES, OR A DRAMATIC EXPRESSION OF EMOTION.

OFF

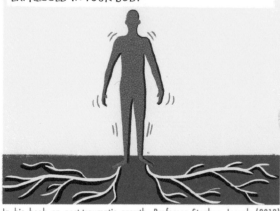

THE KEY SKILL IS SLOWLY LEARNING TO STAY GROUNDED IN THE FACE OF INTENSE SENSATIONS ASSOCIATED WITH OUR BODY'S FEAR RESPONSES EXPRESSED IN YOUR BODY.

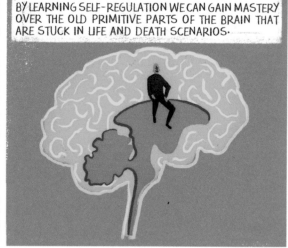

BY LEARNING SELF-REGULATION WE CAN GAIN MASTERY OVER THE OLD PRIMITIVE PARTS OF THE BRAIN THAT ARE STUCK IN LIFE AND DEATH SCENARIOS.

In his book on post-traumatic growth, Professor Stephen Joseph (2013) states that 'On average, only 8–12 per cent of people exposed to traumatic events – and around a fifth to a quarter of those involved in profoundly traumatic experiences – ever reach the diagnostic threshold for PTSD.'

'I believe that the people who are the most resilient, and find the greatest peace in their lives, have learned to tolerate extreme sensations while gaining the capacity for reflective self-awareness' (Levine 2010). Quote on previous page is from the founder of TRE, Berceli 2008b.

TO HEAL TRAUMA WE DO NOT NEED TO UNDERSTAND AND WE DO NOT NEED TO REMEMBER. THIS IS A RADICAL AND STRANGE CONCEPT.

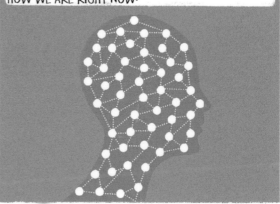

WE CANNOT POSSIBLY UNDERSTAND ALL THE THINGS THAT HAVE HAPPENED TO US. OUT OF THE MILLION (MILLION AND ONE?) EVENTS IN OUR LIVES, WE ARE VERY BRAVE IF WE PICK ONE THING AS THE CAUSE OF HOW WE ARE RIGHT NOW.

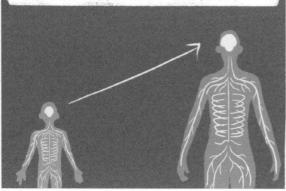

MANY EARLY DEFINING EVENTS WILL NEVER BE BROUGHT INTO THE LIGHT OF CONSCIOUS AWARNESS, BUT THEY SHAPE US NEVERTHELESS. THEY OFTEN UNDERLIE HOW WE RESPOND IN THE PRESENT.

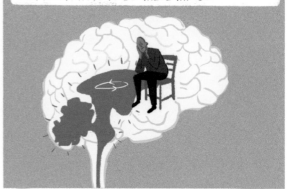

PLEASE DON'T TRY TOO HARD TO THINK OR RATIONALIZE YOUR WAY OUT OF TRAUMA. THE OLD PARTS OF THE BRAIN THAT DEAL WITH TRAUMA DO NOT KNOW HOW TO DO THESE THINGS.

BUT WE CAN USE OUR BODY AND SENSES TO FEEL AND ORIENT OUR WAY OUT OF DANGER. BODY UP, RATHER THAN EGO DOWN.

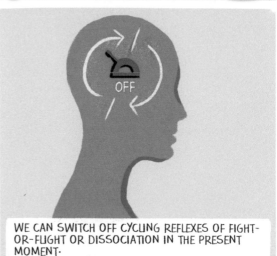

WE CAN SWITCH OFF CYCLING REFLEXES OF FIGHT-OR-FLIGHT OR DISSOCIATION IN THE PRESENT MOMENT.

'In the initial stages of restorative work, bottom-up processing needs to be standard operating procedure' (Levine 2010). Talking can be an important part of healing, but you as a whole organism do not truly change until your body comes to life and comes out of danger mode.

Many therapists are puzzled by clients whose early, unknown developmental history taught them to dissociate. This is coupled with a host of confusing physical and emotional symptoms leaking into their lives that can, however, be traced back to over-activated threat defense strategies.

LET'S LOOK MORE AT HOW THE BRAIN WORKS. SO FAR WE HAVE USED THE TERM 'OLD PARTS OF THE BRAIN' TO DESCRIBE THE REGIONS THAT TRIGGER SURVIVAL RESPONSES.

A SIMPLE BUT USEFUL MODEL IS THE 'TRIUNE (THREE-PART) BRAIN'.

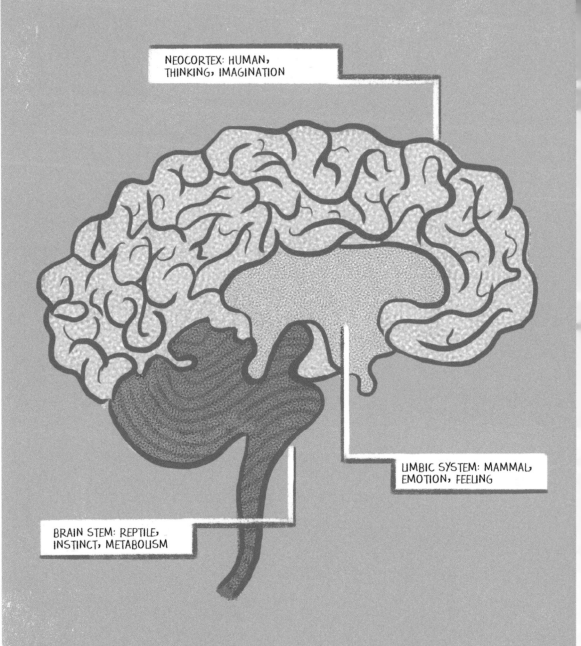

NEOCORTEX: HUMAN, THINKING, IMAGINATION

LIMBIC SYSTEM: MAMMAL, EMOTION, FEELING

BRAIN STEM: REPTILE, INSTINCT, METABOLISM

We can also talk of a 'critter brain' (Jacobs 2012), equivalent to the brain stem and limbic system. Other models are 'rational brain versus emotional brain' (van der Kolk 2014), 'thinking fast and slow' (Kahneman 2011) or simply conscious versus unconscious.

The triune brain model was developed by neuroscientist Paul Maclean in the 1960s. 'This three-layered conceptualization helps us grasp the overall function of higher brain areas better than any other scheme yet devised' (Panksepp 1998).

ONLY TWO PRIMITIVE REFLEXES FOR SURVIVAL HAVE BEEN NAMED IN PREVIOUS PAGES - 'FIGHT-OR-FLIGHT'

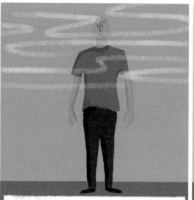

AND DISSOCIATION.

IN FACT, THERE IS AN ADDITIONAL RESPONSE,

'ORIENTATION'. OUR FIRST INSTINCT IS TO CHECK WHAT IS HAPPENING WITH OTHER PEOPLE AND TO SENSE THE SPACE AROUND US.

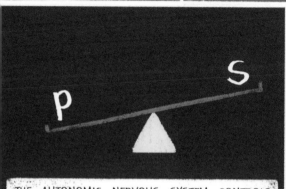

THE AUTONOMIC NERVOUS SYSTEM CONTROLS OUR ORGANS AND METABOLISM. THE AUTONOMICS CONSIST OF PARASYMPATHETICS, MAINLY THE VAGUS NERVE, TO PROMOTE REST AND DIGEST, AND THE SYMPATHETICS TO PROMOTE SPEEDING UP.

WE NOW KNOW THAT THERE ARE TWO CONTROL SYSTEMS FOR THE VAGUS - THE NEW VAGUS AND THE OLD VAGUS.

THE NEW VAGUS OPTIMIZES OXYGEN VIA HEART AND LUNG ACTIVITY AND LINKS WITH OTHER NERVES TO ENGAGE OUR SENSES AND ENHANCE OUR NECK, JAW, FACE AND THROAT MUSCLES.

THE OLD VAGUS IMMOBILIZES US.

HAPPY, HEALTHY PEOPLE, TRUSTED BY OTHERS, HAVE INCREASED NEW VAGUS FIRING. HAPPINESS IS BEING A 'VAGAL SUPERSTAR'.

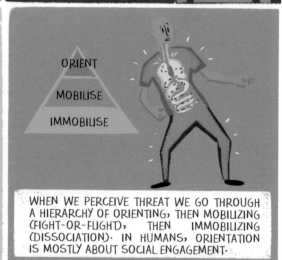

ORIENT

MOBILISE

IMMOBILISE

WHEN WE PERCEIVE THREAT WE GO THROUGH A HIERARCHY OF ORIENTING, THEN MOBILIZING (FIGHT-OR-FLIGHT), THEN IMMOBILIZING (DISSOCIATION). IN HUMANS, ORIENTATION IS MOSTLY ABOUT SOCIAL ENGAGEMENT.

Professor Stephen Porges (2011) developed 'polyvagal theory'. It explains how social interactions are essential negotiations in helping brains find safety. Emotion researcher Dacher Keltner (2009) coined the term 'vagal superstars'.

Orientation, seeking social engagement, is a powerful first response humans have to threat. We learn safety from caregivers. Think of a crying baby: the soft voice, slow, gentle touch and eye contact from their mother, and simply being in that relationship, all switch off the alarm systems.

IN A SAFE, HAPPY MOUSE, ACTIVITY IS MODULATED BY THE NEW VAGUS. IT ACTS AS A BRAKE ON THE SYMPATHETIC NERVOUS SYSTEM.

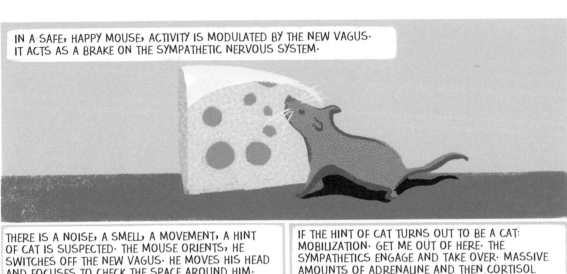

THERE IS A NOISE, A SMELL, A MOVEMENT, A HINT OF CAT IS SUSPECTED. THE MOUSE ORIENTS, HE SWITCHES OFF THE NEW VAGUS. HE MOVES HIS HEAD AND FOCUSES TO CHECK THE SPACE AROUND HIM.

IF THE HINT OF CAT TURNS OUT TO BE A CAT: MOBILIZATION. GET ME OUT OF HERE. THE SYMPATHETICS ENGAGE AND TAKE OVER. MASSIVE AMOUNTS OF ADRENALINE AND THEN CORTISOL ARE SECRETED.

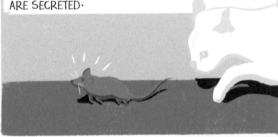

IN HUMANS THE FEEDBACK FROM THE ESCALATING BODY ACTIVITY OF MOBILIZATION WILL BE EMOTIONS AND FEELINGS OF UNEASE-ANXIETY-PANIC (FLIGHT) OR IRRITATION-ANGER-RAGE (FIGHT).

IF MOBILIZATION IS SUCCESSFUL, AND THE MOUSE ESCAPES, IT MAY SHAKE, BREATHE AND REST BEFORE RETURNING TO NEW VAGUS ACTIVITY.

HOWEVER, THE DISCHARGE AND RECOVERY DOES NOT ALWAYS HAPPEN SUCCESSFULLY IN HUMANS.

PEOPLE ARE OFTEN LEFT WITH HEIGHTENED CORTISOL AND SYMPATHETIC ACTIVITY AND THE ASSOCIATED ANGER AND/OR ANXIETY, WHICH CAN LAST, TRAGICALLY, FOR YEARS.

When we are safe and present, our creativity and capacity for love can flourish. The control of our heart and breathing is optimized by the new vagus and we can express our emotions in a wide variety of ways. The new vagus inhibits fear responses (Porges 2011).

An increasing amount of threat begins to change the activity of our bod and our emotional tone. The new vagus begins to fire less – we remove th 'vagal brake' (Thayer and Lane 2000) – and patterns of turning our hea and changing our heart rate emerge, followed by fight-or-flight.

IF THE MOUSE GETS CAUGHT, IT IS INESCAPABLE THREAT. WITH NO ESCAPE OPTIONS, IMMOBILIZING HAS PROVED TO BE A USEFUL EVOLUTIONARY STRATEGY. PLAYING DEAD IS AN OLD VAGUS, REPTILIAN REFLEX.

PREDATORS NEED THE THRILL OF THE STRUGGLE TO STAY ENGAGED. OFTEN CATS LOSE INTEREST AND PAUSE; THIS CAN BE AN OPPORTUNITY FOR THE MOUSE TO MOBILIZE AGAIN.

IF THERE IS NO ESCAPE, THE NATURAL OPIOIDS SECRETED BY THE NERVOUS SYSTEM LIMIT THE PAIN OF DEATH AND INDUCE A DREAMY QUALITY (REMEMBER DAVID LIVINGTONE'S STUPOR).

IN HUMANS, EXCESSIVE OPIOIDS CAN LEAD TO A PLEASANT, SPACEY QUALITY OR A TERRIFYING LOSS OF CONTACT WITH REALITY. THIS CAN BE AN INHERENTLY CONFUSING, FREQUENTLY DEPRESSING, LOST PLACE.

DISSOCIATION IS ONE OF THE BIGGEST PRECURSORS TO GETTING LOST IN TRAUMA RESPONSES. THE INABILITY TO FEEL THE BODY AND LACK OF CONNECTION TO OUR INTERNAL EXPERIENCE OFTEN LEADS TO PAIN AND DEPRESSION.

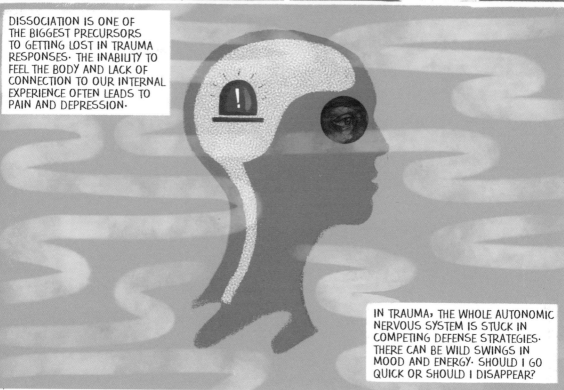

IN TRAUMA, THE WHOLE AUTONOMIC NERVOUS SYSTEM IS STUCK IN COMPETING DEFENSE STRATEGIES. THERE CAN BE WILD SWINGS IN MOOD AND ENERGY. SHOULD I GO QUICK OR SHOULD I DISAPPEAR?

So I leave my body, floating out of it and up to the ceiling, where I watch myself until it becomes too much even from there, and then I fly out of the room, straight to the closed doors and off to safety. It was an inexplicably brilliant feeling' (Rhodes 2015).

An aside: many spiritual seekers mistake endorphin rushes for transcendental experiences – actually they are dissociating. 'Deep embodiment' is a pre-requisite for authentic experiences of 'flow states' and heightened consciousness (Kotler 2013). See also bit.ly/mouse-escape-video.

WE ARE ALWAYS CONSTANTLY UNCONSCIOUSLY SCANNING OUR ENVIRONMENT FOR THREAT.

THE AMYGDALA, A SMALL AREA OF THE LIMBIC SYSTEM, IS THE SMOKE DETECTOR IN OUR NERVOUS SYSTEM.

LIKE MOST SMOKE DETECTORS, IT OFTEN GENERATES AN ALARM AT THE WRONG MOMENT.

THE EXPERIENCE OF TRAUMA CAN BE LIKENED TO THE SIREN GOING OFF, WHEN ALL WE HAVE DONE IS BURNT THE TOAST.

The metaphor of the amygdala as a smoke detector is from van der Kolk (2014). The amygdala 'is part of a threat detection system' (LeDoux 2015). Neuroception is the name for threat detection without awareness. Neuroception 'describes how neural circuits distinguish whether situations o people are safe, dangerous, or life threatening. It explains why a baby co at a care-giver but cries at a stranger' (Porges 2004).

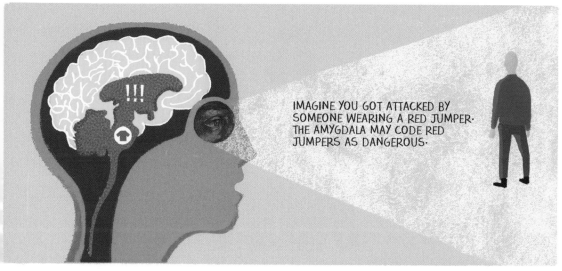

IMAGINE YOU GOT ATTACKED BY SOMEONE WEARING A RED JUMPER. THE AMYGDALA MAY CODE RED JUMPERS AS DANGEROUS.

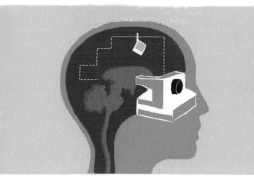

THINK OF THE AMYGDALA AS A POLAROID CAMERA THAT TAKES A SINGLE, BLURRY SNAPSHOT TO RECORD A COMPLEX EXPERIENCE.

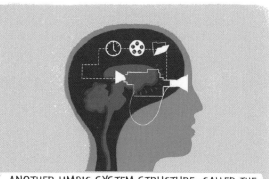

ANOTHER LIMBIC SYSTEM STRUCTURE, CALLED THE HIPPOCAMPUS, SHOULD ENCODE THE TIMELINE AND LINKS TO THE LARGER CONTEXT OF MEMORY. IT TAKES A HIGH MEGAPIXEL, QUALITY VIDEO RECORDING WITH A DATE STAMP.

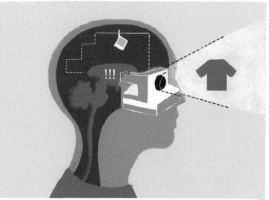

10 YEARS LATER THE AMYGDALA SENSES A RED JUMPER IN THE INCOMING INFORMATION STREAM. THE AMYGDALA GOES CRAZY AND TRIGGERS LIFE OR DEATH RESPONSES.

THAT WAS 10 YEARS AGO.

THE HIPPOCAMPUS SHOULD COME ALONG AND PUT A BRAKE ON, SAYING 'THAT WAS 10 YEARS AGO!' TRAUMA IS A FAILURE OF THE HIGH MEGAPIXEL HIPPOCAMPUS TO UPDATE THE BLURRY POLAROID AMYGDALA TO THE PRESENT.

WE CAN HAVE MANY UNCONSCIOUS TRIGGERS THAT SEND OUR PHYSIOLOGY INTO OVERDRIVE. OH DEAR.

e amygdala helps create 'implicit' memories; for example, conditional arning, gut feelings and riding a bike. The hippocampus should provide timeline and regulate implicit memories, but 'stress hormones (cortisol) ppress the activity of the hippocampus' (Rothschild 2000).

'Prolonged exposure to stress levels of glucocorticoids (cortisol) atrophy hippocampal neuronal processes and, ultimately, cause neuron loss. ... sustained exposure to elevated glucocorticoid concentrations disrupts memory' (Saplosky et al 2000).

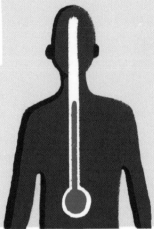

WHAT CAN WE DO TO OVERCOME TRAUMA? THE REST OF THE BOOK EXPLORES TOOLS TO DEVELOP OUR ABILITY TO SELF-REGULATE OUR BODY RESPONSES.

THE FIRST THING TO TAKE ON BOARD IS THE PRINCIPLE OF GOING SLOWLY. HEALTH IS BUILT ONE STEP AT A TIME.

TO QUOTE LAO TZU, 'THE JOURNEY OF A THOUSAND MILES BEGINS WITH ONE STEP.'

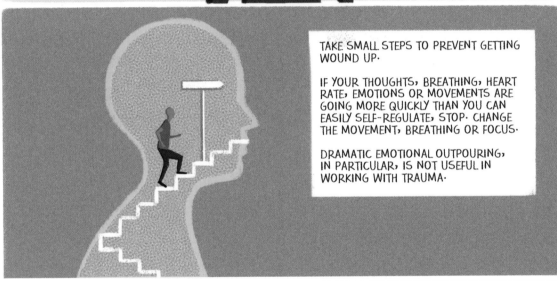

TAKE SMALL STEPS TO PREVENT GETTING WOUND UP.

IF YOUR THOUGHTS, BREATHING, HEART RATE, EMOTIONS OR MOVEMENTS ARE GOING MORE QUICKLY THAN YOU CAN EASILY SELF-REGULATE, STOP. CHANGE THE MOVEMENT, BREATHING OR FOCUS.

DRAMATIC EMOTIONAL OUTPOURING, IN PARTICULAR, IS NOT USEFUL IN WORKING WITH TRAUMA.

GO SLOWLY WITH ANYTHING THAT CAUSES YOU TO FLOAT AWAY.

DISSOCIATION CAN HAPPEN REALLY QUICKLY AND BE QUITE SEDUCTIVE.

BEING IN A BODY CAN BE HARD WORK. IT TAKES PRACTICE TO ACHIEVE EMBODIMENT.

Titration is a concept used by Levine (1997). Titration is a term from chemistry for the slow addition of a known chemical to an unknown solution and the observation of the change. A perfect model, then, for working with the charge of trauma: go slow, take small steps and observe.

'You can be fully in charge of your life only if you acknowledge the real of your body, in all its visceral dimensions'; 'In order to overcome traum you need help to get back in touch with your body, with your Self' (van Kolk 2014).

WORKING WITH TRAUMA IS LIKE BEING AN EXPERT AT OPENING COKE BOTTLES.

TAKE THE TOP OFF TOO QUICKLY AND IT GETS MESSY. DIVE INTO THE TRAUMA STORY TOO QUICKLY AND YOU MAY MEET INTENSE EMOTIONS AND SENSATIONS THAT ARE HARD TO REGULATE.

THE CHARGE INSIDE A BODY WHEN OVERWHELMED CAN BE COMPARED TO A COKE BOTTLE THAT HAS BEEN VIGOROUSLY SHAKEN.

A SMALL OPEN AND A QUICK CLOSE CAN RELIEVE THE PRESSURE. IT MAY TAKE A FEW GOES, BUT IT IS SAFE ONCE YOU GET THE HANG OF IT. AND NO MESS. AND A FULL COKE BOTTLE TO ENJOY.

FINDING SAFETY IS THE KEY TO HEALTH. BRAINS LOVE A SECURE BASE FROM WHICH THEY CAN EXPLORE.

The coke bottle model is from Babette Rothschild (2000). 'Containment, it must be understood, is not suppression; it is rather building a larger, more resilient vessel to hold these difficult affects' (Levine 2010).

'Focus not only on regulating the intense memories activated by trauma but also on restoring a sense of agency, engagement, and commitment through ownership of body and mind' (van der Kolk 2014).

A RESOURCE IS ANYTHING THAT HELPS US FEEL SAFE. ADDING IN THE SENSATIONS ASSOCIATED WITH RESOURCES IS THE BIT THAT MAKES THEM SUCH A POWERFUL TOOL.

MAKE SOME LISTS OF THE THINGS THAT SUPPORT YOU IN LIFE. BE EXPANSIVE. DON'T FORGET YOUR FAVORITE PET - THE UNCONDITIONAL LOVE FROM AN ANIMAL IS OFTEN A FOUNDATION TO BUILD ON.

RIGHT NOW, TRY TO FIND SOME FEELINGS YOU LIKE INSIDE YOU (MY BACK FEELS STRONG; I LIKE MY HANDS; MY NOSE DOES NOT HURT) OR AROUND YOU (THE CHAIR IS WORKING; I CAN SMELL DINNER; THE PICTURE IS GOOD).

IF THAT IS TOO HARD, TRY TO REMEMBER THE LAST TIME YOU FELT GOOD OR IMAGINE WHAT GOOD WOULD FEEL LIKE. IT COULD BE A WALK YOU DID LAST WEEKEND OR YOUR FAVOURITE HOLIDAY MEMORY. ADD AS MUCH DETAIL AS YOU CAN - PUSH YOURSELF.

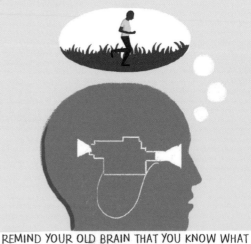

REMIND YOUR OLD BRAIN THAT YOU KNOW WHAT GOODNESS AND SAFETY FEELS LIKE. MAKE THE HIPPOCAMPUS (THE HIGH-QUALITY VIDEO CAMERA) REPLAY SOME GREAT OLD MOVIES.

Professional help and support groups can be essential to provide stability in difficult times. Resources and help can come in many forms. Perserverance and hope in seeking the right way for you to be supported is difficult, but the payoff can be enormous.

'I don't think patients, survivors, victimized people can recover in isolation. They need other people and they need to take action in affiliation with others.' The antidote to 'the abuse of power and authority' is the 'solidarity of resistance' (Herman 2000).

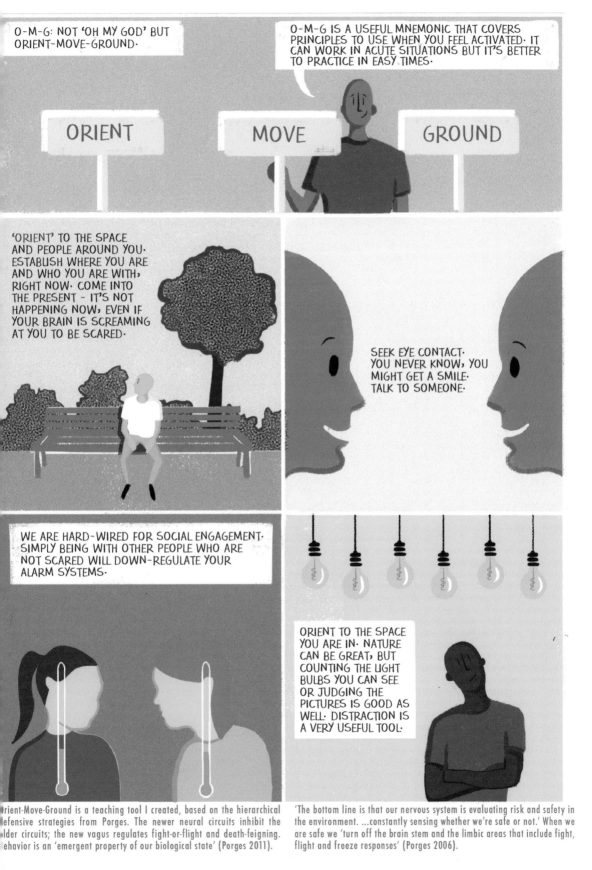

O-M-G: NOT 'OH MY GOD' BUT ORIENT-MOVE-GROUND.

O-M-G IS A USEFUL MNEMONIC THAT COVERS PRINCIPLES TO USE WHEN YOU FEEL ACTIVATED. IT CAN WORK IN ACUTE SITUATIONS BUT IT'S BETTER TO PRACTICE IN EASY TIMES.

ORIENT

MOVE

GROUND

'ORIENT' TO THE SPACE AND PEOPLE AROUND YOU. ESTABLISH WHERE YOU ARE AND WHO YOU ARE WITH, RIGHT NOW. COME INTO THE PRESENT – IT'S NOT HAPPENING NOW, EVEN IF YOUR BRAIN IS SCREAMING AT YOU TO BE SCARED.

SEEK EYE CONTACT. YOU NEVER KNOW, YOU MIGHT GET A SMILE. TALK TO SOMEONE.

WE ARE HARD-WIRED FOR SOCIAL ENGAGEMENT. SIMPLY BEING WITH OTHER PEOPLE WHO ARE NOT SCARED WILL DOWN-REGULATE YOUR ALARM SYSTEMS.

ORIENT TO THE SPACE YOU ARE IN. NATURE CAN BE GREAT, BUT COUNTING THE LIGHT BULBS YOU CAN SEE OR JUDGING THE PICTURES IS GOOD AS WELL. DISTRACTION IS A VERY USEFUL TOOL.

Orient-Move-Ground is a teaching tool I created, based on the hierarchical defensive strategies from Porges. The newer neural circuits inhibit the older circuits; the new vagus regulates fight-or-flight and death-feigning. behavior is an 'emergent property of our biological state' (Porges 2011).

'The bottom line is that our nervous system is evaluating risk and safety in the environment. ...constantly sensing whether we're safe or not.' When we are safe we 'turn off the brain stem and the limbic areas that include fight, flight and freeze responses' (Porges 2006).

'MOVE' TO MAINTAIN CONSCIOUS CONNECTION WITH THE BODY. TRAUMA OFTEN INVOLVES THE BODY BEING STUCK IN INCOMPLETE ACTIONS THAT WERE ABORTED.

WE CONTRACT IN FEAR TO MAKE OURSELVES SMALL, WE EXPAND AND MOVE FORWARDS WHEN WE FEEL SAFE. SO PRACTICE EXPANDING.

VISUALIZING MOVEMENT CAN BE JUST AS GOOD AS ACTUALLY MOVING. BE CREATIVE – IMAGINE RUNNING ON GRASS WITH THE WIND IN YOUR FACE.

START WITH VERY SMALL MOVEMENTS TO ENGAGE THE BODY. WIGGLE YOUR TOES, PUSH YOUR LEGS INTO THE FLOOR, RUB YOUR HANDS TOGETHER.

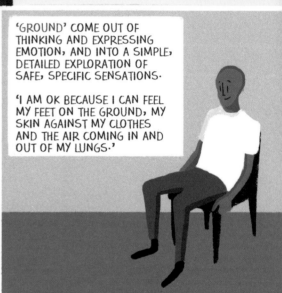

'GROUND' COME OUT OF THINKING AND EXPRESSING EMOTION, AND INTO A SIMPLE, DETAILED EXPLORATION OF SAFE, SPECIFIC SENSATIONS.

'I AM OK BECAUSE I CAN FEEL MY FEET ON THE GROUND, MY SKIN AGAINST MY CLOTHES AND THE AIR COMING IN AND OUT OF MY LUNGS.'

IN DISSOCIATION THERE IS A LOSS OF THE ABILITY TO CLEARLY FEEL THE SHAPE, SIZE AND WEIGHT OF THE BODY. DO NOT TRY TO CHANGE THE SPEEDY, TIGHT, PAINFUL BITS OF YOUR BODY. FOCUS ON FEELING THE ABSENT, HAZY, HARD-TO-FEEL BITS.

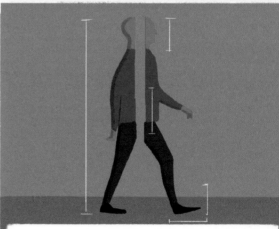

PRACTICE HAVING A FRONT AND A BACK, NOTICE IF YOU FEEL INSIDE OR OUTSIDE YOUR BODY, CHECK THE SIZE OF YOUR FEET AND THE FEELING OF YOUR LOWER BELLY. THE MORE DETAIL YOU CAN FIND THE BETTER.

Levine (2010) is very keen on completing the 'instinctual imperative that was thwarted... We have to help clients discover just where in her body she readied for action, and which action had been blocked in its execution.' We are left braced or collapsed in trauma.

'"Grounded" means that you can feel your butt in your chair, see the light coming through the window, feel the tension in your calves, and hear the wind stirring in the tree outside' (van der Kolk 2014). Check the wonderful Amy Cuddy (2012) TED talk on making yourself big.

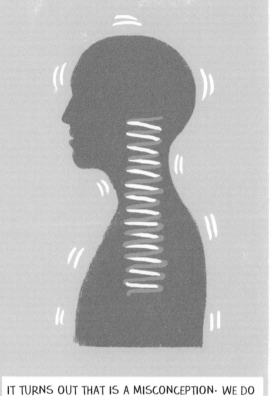

SHAKING IS SOMETHING THAT HAS TRADITIONALLY BEEN SEEN AS A SYMPTOM AND AS A PATHOLOGICAL RESULT OF TRAUMA.

IT TURNS OUT THAT IS A MISCONCEPTION. WE DO NOT SHAKE BECAUSE WE ARE TRAUMATIZED, WE SHAKE BECAUSE IT IS A NATURAL MECHANISM IN THE BODY TO OPTIMIZE TENSION.

TRY TO STAND PERFECTLY STILL. IT IS NOT POSSIBLE. OUR MUSCLES ARE CONSTANTLY CHANGING THEIR TONE AS WE DANCE WITH GRAVITY. LOW LEVEL OSCILLATIONS IN POSTURAL MUSCLES (A FANCY WAY OF SAYING SHAKING) IS NORMAL.

IF WE ARE STRESSED WE DO NOT CONTROL THESE TREMORS VERY ACCURATELY. SOMETIMES THEY GO INTO A POSITIVE FEEDBACK LOOP AND WE VISIBLY SHAKE A LOT.

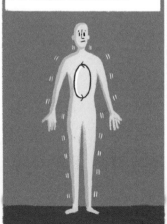

HOWEVER, IF WE CAN BE CURIOUS ABOUT TREMORS AND INTERACT WITH THEM, THE INFORMATION FLOW BETWEEN MUSCLES AND NERVOUS SYSTEM HELPS THE BRAIN RESET THE TONE IN MUSCLES. SHAKING CAN DISCHARGE EXCESS TENSION AND WAKE UP FROZEN BITS OF THE BODY.

TRE is a wonderful self-regulation tool devised by Dr David Berceli. He discovered a simple way to self induce therapeutic tremors. 'Exercises that produce tremors bypass the thinking brain, giving us direct access to the unconscious reptilian brain' (Berceli 2008a).

In TRE a series of seven exercises tire out some of the big muscles in the hips. With encouragement, practice and curiosity it is possible to turn on and turn off shaking in the pelvis and, eventually, all over the body. The tremors in TRE help to reboot the nervous system.

THE VERY NATURE OF TRAUMA IS THAT IT IS OVERWHELMING. IT IS MORE THAN THE ORGANISM CAN COPE WITH.

TRAUMA SHATTERS OUR WORLD VIEW. RULES OF FAIRNESS AND JUSTICE NO LONGER SEEM TO APPLY. TRAUMA OFTEN LEADS TO A SPIRITUAL CRISIS AND A PROFOUND RE-EVALUATION OF MEANING.

TRAUMA TAKES US TO VERY PRIMITIVE PLACES OF FIGHT-OR-FLIGHT OR DISSOCIATION. IT IS VERY HARD TO LIVE FULLY WITH OUR BRAIN SCREAMING 'DANGER!' AND GENERATING LIFE OR DEATH SCENARIOS AT THE SLIGHTEST STIMULUS.

IT IS REALLY IMPORTANT TO FIND A COMMUNITY AND GET SUPPORT TO REDISCOVER WHAT SAFETY FEELS LIKE. TAKE SOME CHANCES AND OPEN UP TO YOUR FRIENDS AND LOVED ONES.

THE MODEL OFFERED HERE IS THAT INHERENT WITHIN YOU IS THE ABILITY TO SWITCH OFF OVERACTIVE PROTECTIVE REFLEXES. YOU ARE NOT MAD OR BROKEN.

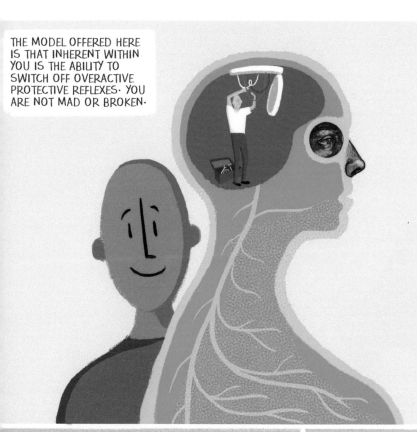

RECALIBRATING THE SMOKE DETECTOR OF THE AMYGDALA IS A GREAT START TO HEALING TRAUMA.

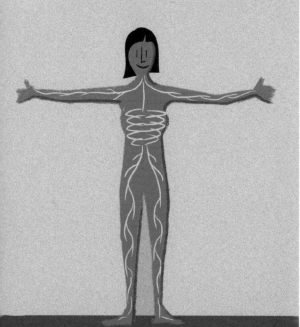

WHATEVER YOUR BELIEF SYSTEM ON MEANING AND PURPOSE IN LIFE, THERE IS THE VERY SIMPLE FACT OF THE BODY. YOU ARE IN A BODY RIGHT NOW. LEARN HOW IT WORKS AND EMBRACE THE MESSY, EARTHY GROUND OF FEELING.

LOSING CONTACT WITH YOUR BODY, AND YOUR ABILITY TO FEEL THE JOY AND GOODNESS INSIDE YOU, IS NOT A PRICE WORTH PAYING, WHATEVER HAS BEEN DONE TO YOU.

STRESS AND TRAUMA CHANGE HOW OUR BRAINS WORK. SQUEEZE ANY HUMAN HARD ENOUGH AND WE WILL BE OVERWHELMED. OFTEN WE DO NOT KNOW WHICH EXPERIENCES IMPRINTED OUR NERVOUS SYSTEM.

THE BEST WAY TO RESET THE OLD PARTS OF OUR BRAIN IS TO SLOWLY WAKE UP THE BODY. HEALING TRAUMA IS NOT ABOUT REMEMBERING, IT IS ABOUT SELF-REGULATING TO TURN DOWN INTENSE REACTIONS IN THE BODY.

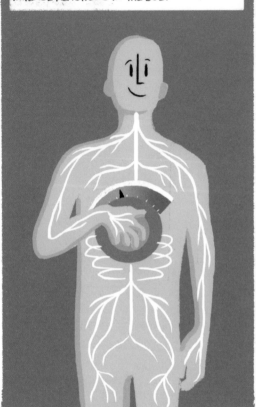

BEING IN A BODY, WITHOUT CHRONIC TENSION PATTERNS AND A SENSITIZED BRAIN, WILL LEAD US TO BEING HAPPIER AND HEALTHIER.